c

THE STORY OF
LACE and EMBROIDERY

MAISON DE LA BRODERIE ET DE LA DENTELLES PARIS

The Story of
Lace and Embroidery

by

DAVID E. SCHWAB

FAIRCHILD PUBLICATIONS INC., NEW YORK 3, N.Y.

PRINTED IN THE UNITED STATES OF AMERICA

Acknowledgment

It seems proper here to acknowledge the helpful efforts in connection with this book on the part of the following: La Maison de la Dentelle et de la Broderie, Paris, France, "Appenzellerland," Gais, Switzerland, Armand Schwab, Jr., who read the manuscript, and various other sources whose contributions are credited within the book.

Dedicated with affection

to

My dear wife, Pearl R. Schwab

My source of inspiration in every endeavor.

Introduction

Lace, the dictionary tells us, is "a delicate openwork fabric, usually figured, of fine threads." The earliest users of lace might not have given the exact definition, but they would probably have felt about lace as people do now. There has been a remarkable continuity of interest in lace—a warm feeling for this fabric which is almost a synonym for grace, delicacy and good taste. This feeling has lasted despite large changes in its manufacture and use.

For hundreds of years after its birth, lace was made only by hand. Its creation then was more than a trade; it was very nearly a fine art. The beauties and distinctions of the various laces were known and understood by the great ladies and gentlemen who wore them, much as a connoisseur knows a fine painting.

But lace was expensive; it was a luxury fabric, and few could afford it. It was natural to treat it as a collector's item.

Today, with the advent of machine-made lace, we tend to treat this queen of all the textiles with less reverence. For lace is within everyone's reach. It is a strong, practical material. You see it on babies' clothes, on lingerie, on formal gowns, on handkerchiefs.

But you notice, perhaps, that all laces are not the same. Is there, perhaps, a special lace type for every specialized purpose? There is—and knowing something of the history, tradition, and classification of lace adds to the fascination of wearing it.

The History

Evidence exists that, at the summit of their cultures, the ancient Chinese, Egyptians, Persians and Greeks made a kind of lace. We know little, however, about the composition or appearance of their version.

The history of lace, as we know it, really starts in Italy, where the fabric was produced prior to the sixteenth century. Venice, fabulous seat of so much Rennaissance grandeur, taught hand lace-making to other sections of Italy, and from there it spread to France, Flanders, Belgium, England and Ireland. Italy, however, seemed to be especially fitted by temperament, taste and talent for the cultivation of this new art. At first, lace-making was a pastime for gentlewomen with delicate hands, who devoted their leisure, sentiment and artistic leanings to creating rich designs and executing them. They taught the nuns, whose lives of seclusion gave them ample time to study and develop the delicate art. From these sources the art spread through the country. The people of Italy learned to make lace. Workshops were established, and from them soon arose the famous songs of the Italian lace-makers. A new art-craft joined the distinguished list of Italian exports in the sixteenth century.

The advent of lace caught the fancy of men and women. It was glorified in literature and in art. Paintings and portraits by the world's greatest painters—Raphael, Franz Hals, and Velasquez—featured lace ruffs, guimpes, and headdresses on distinguished men and women. These paintings teach us most of what we know of the costumes of the period. It is interesting to note that it was in

No. 1
HANDMADE POINT VENICE

Needlepoint lace, Italian XVII Century, flat Venice type.
THE METROPOLITAN MUSEUM OF ART

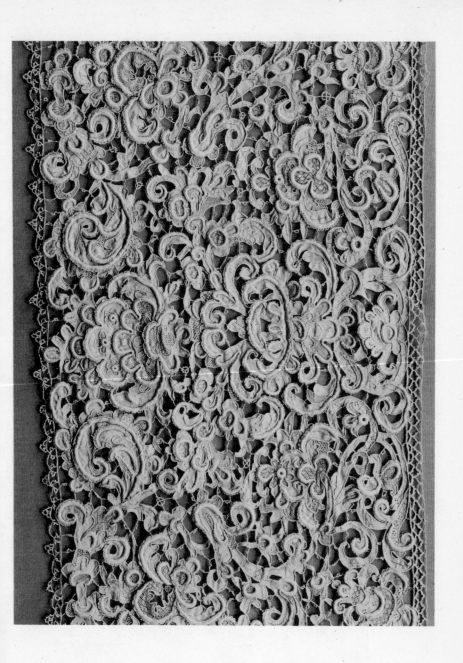

No. 2
HANDMADE GROS POINT DE VENICE

Heavy Venetian Point, Italian XVII Century.
THE METROPOLITAN MUSEUM OF ART

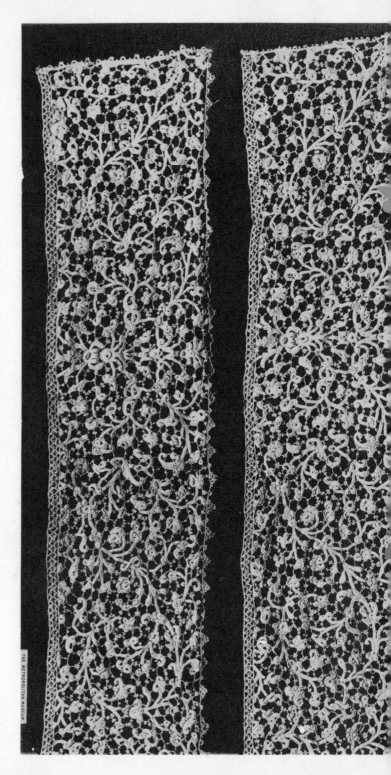

No. 3
HANDMADE ROSALINE

Needlepoint lace, Italian XVII Century, second half.
Light weight Venice.

THE METROPOLITAN MUSEUM OF ART

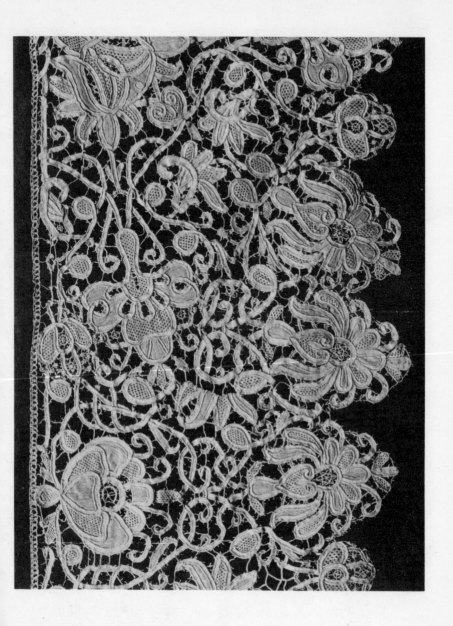

No. 4
HANDMADE ANTIQUE BURANO

Needlepoint lace, Italian XVII Century, Tape and Needlepoint
(Mezzo Punto).
THE METROPOLITAN MUSEUM OF ART

precisely the two countries where art flourished most at this time, Flanders and Italy, that lace-making achieved its earliest perfection.

In all the countries of Europe, the wealthiest and most distinguished families came to look upon lace as a proud possession; it was a mark of prosperity. The fabulously wealthy Doges, whose ships took the treasures of Italy all over the Mediterranean area, the powerful Medici family and others led in the extravagant purchase of laces. So extravagant were they, in fact, that laws were decreed forbidding the purchase of laces exceeding certain specified sums. Masterpieces made into altar covers and robes for distinguished men of the Church became sacred treasures in cathedrals, and were collected and preserved in museums.

The great skill and sentiment which characterized this work raised lace-making to a pinnacle of richness in the seventeenth century. Lace thus played a role during the period of greatest intellectual and artistic development, the Renaissance period.

Lace came to France with Catherine de Medici. This arbiter of Italian fashion became the consort of King Henry II of France in 1533, and brought to her new country the art of lace-making. Venetian experts in the craft were brought to France and found apt pupils. The French royal court, always known for its gaiety and elegance, became the key source of inspiration for lace modes. While Venice was to remain the undisputed center for the heavier type of "needle" or "point" lace ("Venice lace"), it was France which responded to a demand for lighter types by providing laces of new grace and delicacy. Among these were Alencon, Argentan and Chantilly. Worn as cravats and ruffles by men, used for fans, handkerchief borders and gowns by women, these new laces added allure to elegance; lace became the fabric of romance, as well as of dignity.

Lace, by now, had become an important factor in world trade. Regions and countries vied with each other in attempts to create new patterns and methods which would bring a higher demand for their own output. New designs and stitches were worked out and their secrets jealously guarded. So important did lace become that

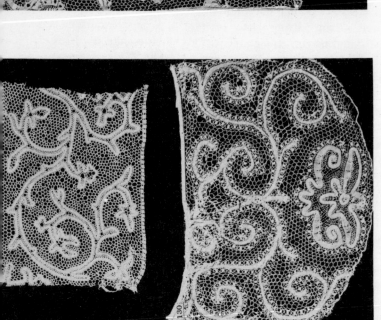

No. 5

HANDMADE POINT DE MILAN

Bobbin lace, Flemish XVII-XVIII Centuries. The origin is Italian.

ambassadors in foreign capitals were given the additional duty of reporting on developments in the lace industries of the countries to which they were assigned. As new designs were produced, each became identified with the country or city of its origin. Thus were born the names which soon were repeated throughout the world, and which are still in use today: Point Burano, Point Venice, Point Milan, Point de France, Point de Bruxelles, Point d'Angleterre, Point d'Espagne . . . and the lighter types—Point de Paris, Point d'Alencon, Point d'Argentan, Point Duchesse, Chantilly, Valenciennes, and Mechlin.

Flanders and Belgium moved into a leading position in the development of hand-made laces during the sixteenth century. As the years passed they made their own contribution to the art. The eighteenth century saw the zenith of this region's glory, when Belgium and Flanders enjoyed a thriving industry in laces made by hand. Evidence of their contribution can be found in the museum in Brussels—Point d'Angleterre of rare delicacy, exquisite bedspreads, and magnificent garments for church dignitaries. Brussels or Brabant Lace, Lace of Flanders, Mechlin, Valenciennes and Binche owe either their origin or their development to the instinct and techniques of Belgian workers. Belgium, particularly the towns of Lierre and Bruges, became famous for laces of its own particular kind, which have maintained this reputation through centuries. By the end of the sixteenth century the making of pillow lace had been introduced to the Harz Mountain region of Germany. It was brought there by a woman named Barbara Uttman, who learned it in Flanders and taught it to help her neighbors.

It was during the reign of Queen Elizabeth that close relations between the courts of France and England brought the glamor of beautiful lace to Britain for elaborate neck ruffs, aprons, gowns and the more recently introduced lace handkerchief. The accomplished Queen was known for her large wardrobe, which included elaborate gowns for court functions. As a result, the use of lace became very prominent in England, reflecting the trend of fashion in France. Two groups of workers arrived to help—French lace-

No. 7
HANDMADE POINT DE GAZE

Needlepoint lace, Belgian (Brussels), second half of XIX Century.
These were also made in Italy.
THE METROPOLITAN MUSEUM OF ART

No. 8
HANDMADE POINT DE GAZE

Handkerchief border needlepoint lace, Belgian (Brussels),
late XIX Century.
THE METROPOLITAN MUSEUM OF ART

Spain now developed its own distinctive types, influenced in many cases by the intricacies of Moorish art. To certain types the name of Point d'Espagne was given. Spain's particular genius was shown in the characteristic mantilla, the favorite headdress of all Spanish women. Elaborate pieces were worn at social affairs; the mantilla was *de rigueur* at court and was the symbol of gaiety at fiestas. It was, and still is, used also by women to cover the neck and arms at church.

When Louis XIV married the Infanta of Spain, daughter of King Philip, the Spanish aristocracy got a look at the extravagant use of lace at formal functions of the court of France. This proved a stimulus to the fabric in Spain. Gowns with three tiers of wide laces on the skirts, and rows and rows of overlapping lace edges forming puffed sleeves, became the fashion. Spain began making the beautiful laces of the lighter types, which had been created by France.

Later, under King Louis XVI and his brilliant Queen, Marie Antoinette, the French court went into its dizzy death dance leading to the French Revolution, dressed in lace. The pleasure-loving Queen was conspicious in the social life of Paris, as well as at the functions of the court itself; gowns of lace were her favorites, and the world followed her lead.

It was at this point that the events of history brought lace even to the wilderness shores of America. For during this period, Benjamin Franklin arrived in Paris representing the American Colonies. He secured recognition by France and got French aid to help America achieve independence—guns, clothing, money and men, sent under the leadership of Lafayette and Rochambeau. After the war, officers of the French expedition remained concentrated in the coastal towns, particularly in Newport, Rhode Island, the headquarters of the fleet. They stimulated the colonials' social life; with victory achieved, there ensued a period of gaiety and chivalry, and Newport adopted some of the social customs of Paris. It was natural that American women should reach out for finery of every sort, especially from France. Lace with its enchantment was brought to the New World to beautify the home and milady's wardrobe,

No. 9
HANDMADE POINT D'ALENCON

Needlepoint lace, French XVII-XIX Century. A most popular lace in all widths.

THE METROPOLITAN MUSEUM OF ART

No. 10
HANDMADE POINT D'ARGENTAN

Needlepoint lace, French mid-XIX Century,
very similar to Alencon.
THE METROPOLITAN MUSEUM OF ART

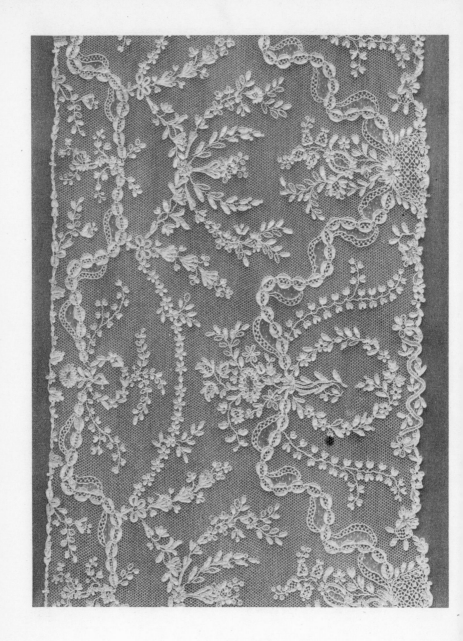

No. 11
HANDMADE POINT D'ARGENTAN

Needlepoint lace, French mid-XIX Century,
very similar to Alencon.
THE METROPOLITAN MUSEUM OF ART

No. 12
HANDMADE POINT DE FRANCE

Needlepoint lace, French, first half of the XVIII Century.
THE METROPOLITAN MUSEUM OF ART

and a new, large and affluent society fell slave to the charm of lace. Meanwhile, in the southern states, French settlers established lace as a favorite material and adornment, which it remains to this day.

Elaborate gowns, the product of the French couture, now revealed lace at its most charming. Fashions were spread by a precursor of today's women's magazine—the fashion doll. Paris had for years sent these elaborately dressed mannequins throughout the world. They were received, in far-off cities, as the latest creations from the cosmopolitan center of fashion and elegance, and the new vogues were copied hastily. Lace was soon the leading fabric for the wardrobe of these dolls and thus the fame and beauty of its delicate textures were spread far and wide.

After the French Revolution, the courts of the two Napoleons kept lace a favorite, but the time was fast drawing near when the rapid development of machine laces would present a serious threat to the hand industry. Napoleon I, after his marriage to Marie Louise, is known to have ordered a complete set of bed and pillow covers made of luxurious Alencon lace, with the Napoleonic cipher, in the form of a bee, woven into each article. The Emperor's son received an outfit made of Alencon which, with Chantilly, was reputed to be Napoleon's favorite lace. He encouraged and decreed the wearing of lace at his court, and bestowed favors on the people who made the fabric.

Later, at the coronation of England's Queen Victoria, the new Queen wore a handsome lace dress, the material for which was said to have cost £1,000.

Perhaps the most magnificent single lace dress we know of was the one given by Napoleon III to the Empress Eugenie. Its cost is said to have been 200,000 francs—equal, then, to $40,000. It required the labor of thirty-six women, working for eighteen months. The world's best-dressed woman at that time, the Empress particularly loved all types of lace. She made a point of buying and encouraging her friends to buy the hand-made varieties, for by her time the machine-made substitutes had succeeded in making heavy inroads on the old art.

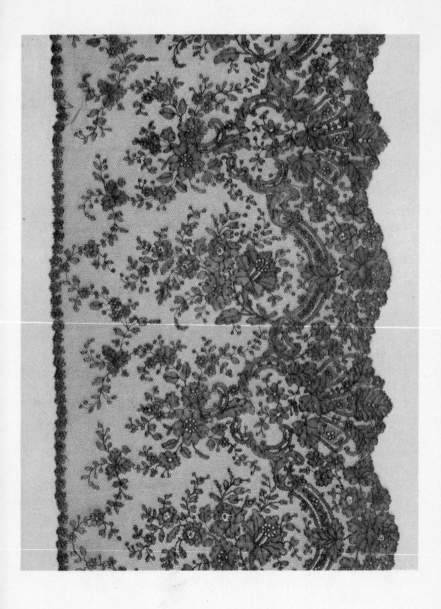

No. 13
HANDMADE CHANTILLY LACE

Bobbin lace, French, second half of the XIX Century.
THE METROPOLITAN MUSEUM OF ART

The Empress Eugenie, frantically buying up hand-made lace, may be taken as the symbol of the end of an era in lace-making, as well as of French and world social history. The great days of pillow and needle lace were drawing to a close. More and more people were buying the new product of the machine lace industry, which was rapidly becoming more efficient and developing finer patterns. The creative spirit was largely transferred to mechanical ingenuity and machine lace, as we shall see, was to become a mass product of beauty and utility to a degree heretofore undreamed of.

Despite the quantitative leadership of the machine industry today, hand-made lace still survives as a living art, particularly in Belgium, France, Italy and China.

Belgium

The Belgians, who displayed a genius rivalling that of Venice in the earliest development of lace, play a vital role in the preservation of lace-making by hand. Flax grown in Belgium has given an added advantage and incentive to the Belgian worker. Well-organized schools, mostly in convents, continue to teach the art as a means of livelihood in modern times. The present lace workers of Belgium have turned profitably to such articles as tablecloths, bedspreads, handkerchiefs and collars, of which many beautiful specimens are offered throughout the world.

Types of laces made by hand with machine-made lace as background material, specifically the well-known Princess Lace and Milan Lace, a finer type made with tape as part of the design, are permitted to be sold in Belgium as "real" lace. On the other hand, the similarity of machine-made reproductions of real Binche, Bruges, Alencon, Venice and others is at times so great that Belgian laws require a guarantee as to the authenticity of laces sold as "hand-made."

What is called Point de Flandre in French, Flemish Point in English, Punto Piamengla in Italian, and marketed at times as Point d'Angleterre, is the original creation of the Belgians. It re-

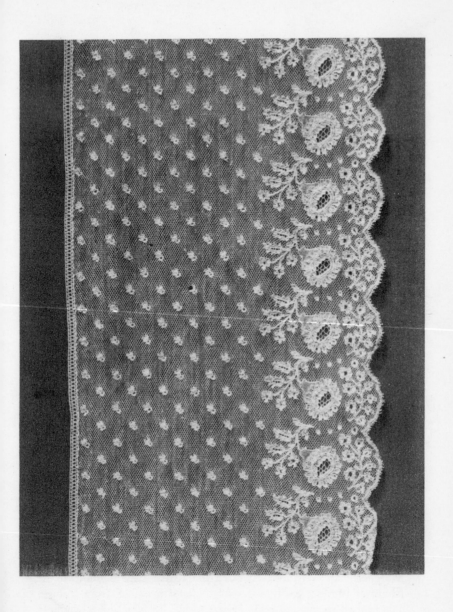

No. 14
HANDMADE MECHLIN

Bobbin lace, Flemish, about 1800-1825.
THE METROPOLITAN MUSEUM OF ART

mains the indigenous needle lace of Belgium. In addition, the famous hand-made laces of Italian, French and English origin are today also made by Belgian artisans.

France

In France the hand craft goes on too, with needle lace-making taught at a school in Alencon. Point d'Alencon remains the high luxury lace for those who can afford it, particularly for the finest lingerie and where light laces are required. The city of Argentan teaches, in its convents, the making of its own kind of light lace, less expensive, useful for rich household decorations.

In Bayeux, in the Department of Calvados, a considerable number of women still work on hand laces, placing bobbins and twisting threads together on pin cushions to make a pillow lace at reasonable cost. At LePuy laces made by hand are similar to the Cluny and Torchon types. They are imitated on the braiding or "Barmen" machine, which provides a larger supply than would otherwise be possible, and are used primarily for household purposes.

Lyons makes the so-called "hand-run" Alencons. The background of this lace is a machine-made "shadow lace," with the flowers and wreaths woven in. On this surface a pusher machine, controlled by hand, imposes the characteristic *cordonnet* of Alencon.

Italy

In Italy, the cradle of lace-making, Venice remains the champion of the industry. Its palaces offer a wealth of *chef d'oeuvres* from the families with which they were associated. Naples, in the south, displays the beautiful work of Italy's southern workers.

The revival of lace-making was especially promoted by Queen Margherita of Italy. She founded the Royal Lace School on the Island of Burano, easily accessible by steam launch from Venice. The school has made steady efforts to inspire new and reasonably priced articles. The main present-day product is still typically Venetian—Point de Venice.

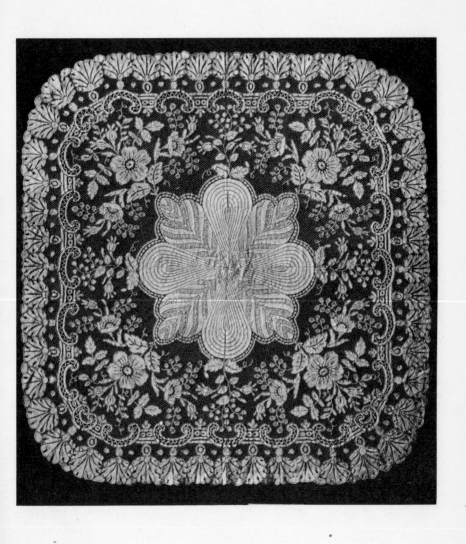

No. 15
HANDMADE VALENCIENNE

Handkerchief border is bobbin Belgian lace of the XIX Century.
THE METROPOLITAN MUSEUM OF ART

With their superior agility, these well-trained workers also create needlepoint laces resembling Alencon and Brussels lace of fine, light texture. Exhibitions in Venice showing how these laces are made and generous displays throughout Italy have achieved the gratifying result of perpetuating the fame of the Italian craftswoman.

No. 16A

*Pillow lace worker making Cluny lace. The carved wooden bobbins
are heavily weighted at the bottom in order to pull the threads taut.
The woman is wearing a cap of lace of finer quality, probably Lille
or Point de Paris, made by herself on the same pillow.*

MAISON DE LA BRODERIE ET DE LA DENTELLES PARIS

No. 16B

The lace-maker is at work on needle point lace, Rose Point, Brussels needle point, or Point de Gaze, three names for one lace. The pattern, drawn on parchment, is attached to two layers of linen to make a firm solid surface to work on.

MAISON DE LA BRODERIE ET DE LA DENTELLES PARIS

Lace Made by Machine

During the latter half of the eighteenth century, mechanical substitutes were taking the place of handwork in one textile field after the other: the Industrial Revolution was stirring. Lace machines came too. Here, as usual, technical invention kept pace with demand and economic pressure; there was a large market waiting for lace at a low price.

It was primarily in England that the lace machine was developed. It began with the old stocking frame, or knitting machine, which was modified finally to turn out a lacy material. In about 1780 net machines were functioning in France and in England. The product of these machines, it was clear at the time, would lead the way toward replacing hand-made lace. In 1802 an Englishman, Robert Brown, turned out an excellent machine that produced nets of all sizes. Net produced in this way was used as a background into which lace designs were worked by hand; machinery had thus gone half way.

Improvements continued on the net machine. Then, in 1809, Heathcoat got a patent for a "bobbin net" machine which was the basis for the real lace machine. In 1813 John Leavers worked out the principles of this machine—one which would produce a fancy pattern at the same time that the background of net was being made. This was the culminating step forward, and the Leavers machine's product was immediately hailed as very close to the real thing. In defiance of laws forbidding the export of lace machines, the Leavers' models, broken down into parts, were smuggled over to France. By 1826 the English patents had expired.

Considerable machines were set up in Calais, France, just across the English Channel, where many Englishmen had settled during the 210 years prior to 1558, when the city was in English hands. It was, furthermore, logical to settle close to Paris, whose authority in fashion was of invaluable assistance.

In 1837, France, by the application of the famous Jacquard Control System to the Leavers machine, achieved the final goal: translation of the most complicated patterns, through a punched-card system, into the proper motions of the machine to reproduce splendid lace designs of hand origin. England promptly adopted this development. Nottingham became headquarters for lace manufacturing, and reached out through a vast system of distribution to bring the product to every corner of the world.

The French industry developed most rapidly. Soon Calais changed its name from *"Clef de France"* ("Key to France") to *"Capitale de la Dentelle"* ("Capital of Lace").

Valenciennes was the type of lace most frequently made on the early machines. However, varied demands, which came chiefly from the couture of Paris, brought about greater versatility and perfection in designing and technical skill. Soon Point de Paris, Alencon, Binche, Chantilly and other types were rolling through the machines, rivaling in delicacy and workmanship the beautiful handicraft of former days.

Many old artisans, or their descendents, were soon engaged in machine lace production. They still loved lace and knew it well, and were determined to keep it the "aristocrat of fabrics" while its lower price brought it a far larger market than had ever been dreamed of. Nottingham and Calais flourished and lace became an important factor in the export trades of France and England.

It is a fascinating experience nowadays to watch a tremendous lace machine at work. Its weight is about 17 tons; it covers about 10 by 50 feet of floor space. The bobbins swing through the threads of the warp, the warp shifts back and forth according to the Jacquard control, and great rolls of lace result. Fine yarns of cotton are most often used, but so are silk, rayon, nylon, wool, metallic

No. 34

THE LEAVERS (Go-Through) LACE MACHINE

*This machine is equipped with Jacquard attachment, making
possible an endless variety of patterns.*
Courtesy of AMERICAN LACE MFRS. ASSN., INC.

threads and many others. In one day such a machine produces a piece of Valenciennes which would have required six months' labor by the most skilled hand-worker. So delicate and perfect is the product that in many cases it is difficult for any but an expert to tell the machine-made from the hand-worked. (Plate 34).

Rapid developments took place in the various supplementary processes of lace-making. Among the necessary procedures, now mostly mechanized, are washing, bleaching, dyeing and finishing, the "drawing" of threads to separate the lace (some of which is done today in the U. S. A. by an acetone separating process) clipping loose threads, and cutting scallops where necessary.

The United States lace industry really got under way only at the beginning of the twentieth century, and then slowly. For a time the export of lace machines was flatly forbidden by England, but many machines were brought to the United States broken down into small parts, which were later assembled by skilled workers, also imported from England. Then, in 1909, after the British ban was lifted, the United States Congress passed a law permitting duty-free importation, for a seventeen-month period, of Leavers machines from England. The machines were expensive and the lifting of the 45 percent duty made it very attractive for prospective manufacturers here to bring over machines.

The industry requires workers of great skill and experience—generally a three-year apprenticeship is necessary.

Protected by tariffs that run from 40 to 90 percent, the industry has grown steadily here, so that its present annual production is now about $30,000,000. The important materials are cotton, both American and English, rayon, silk and, more recently, nylon.

Nottingham, England, Calais and Caudry, France and several areas of the United States are the main centers of machine made laces today. Vienna produces machine lace, as do Italy and Czechoslovakia. Those who design and create machine lace aim at maintaining the allure of the fabric and providing modern woman with a luxury item at prices within the reach of most.

Lace Today

This, then, is the story of lace until now. Clearly this simple, graceful fabric is deeply involved with the whole history of the world's culture and artistic development. Pieces of old lace, exhibited with paintings and sculpture in museums, are sources of continuing pleasure and inspiration.

But what of today? If the clatter of machines has replaced the old ballads sung by Venetian lacemakers, if wide distribution has taken the place of Alencon pillowcases made exclusively by hand for Napoleon, lace is still lace. It is still designed by artists, translated into fabrics by skilled technicians and treated at every stage of manufacture with expert care.

The American woman cherishes the same heritage of beauty that animated the queens and *grandes dames* of past centuries. Women love lace instinctively as something to be cherished; they know well that it is the fabric that most nearly epitomizes feminine charm and loveliness.

Here, in other words, is no ordinary fabric. Its choice and use can be made a rich artistic experience. An intimate knowledge of the names and distinctive features of the various laces adds much to their appreciation and enjoyment.

Embroidery

Embroidery differs from lace in that it is the embellishment, by needlework, of a background fabric such as cotton, linen, net, silk, velvet or others.

Luxurious embroideries made by hand have been found dating back to the eighth century. Egypt, Persia, Syria, Greece and Italy were among the producers. They used cotton, linen, silk or metallic threads to embellish hand-woven cotton and silk fabrics.

In the eleventh and twelfth centuries we get glimpses of elaborate trimming with gold and silver threads in the pages of Dante, who deplored the passing of the days of simple dress in favor of extravagance and luxury. It was about this time that embroidery workers, because of the prohibitive price of gold thread, turned to using flaxen threads on less costly materials. Examples of the work of this period are to be found in museums today.

France soon proved to be a fertile field for embroidery needlework. Its particular contribution has been an inventiveness and ingenuity that has more than once saved the hand embroidery industry from monotonous crystallization.

As early as 1363, craftsmen in Nancy and Luneville began to embroider materials with pearls. In later years scintillant spangles of many hues were invented and were used alone or combined with pearls as a revolutionary new kind of decoration for church and home and women's attire. To the embroiderers, the villagers of the Vosges Mountains, the new craft brought fame and monetary reward.

When silk was introduced into France in the seventeenth century and nets came a century later, these materials served as backgrounds for the embroidery of flowers, leaves, and outlines of pearls and sequins, which still are the leading motifs. At Lyon, silk was embroidered with gold and silver threads, the product becoming known throughout the world.

In the hand-made embroidery field today, Epinal and Luxeuil work principally in white embroidery, with the foliage or feather stitch a specialty. Luxeuil developed a technique of joining embroidery with lace. In Britanny the specialty is white embroidery on net, the original of which has become known as Bretonne lace and is now made in many places by machine. Normandy produces primarily tablecloths and napkins.

As one of the most prevalent of all crafts, embroidery has been developed in many other lands. For centuries, long ago, China found in embroidery one of its most important artistic expressions —rich clothing embellished with silk and, most impressive, decorative panels on which magnificent scenes and designs were "painted" with a needle. Even today, hand embroidery on low-cost backgrounds is one of the important sources of income for large masses in China.

Embroidery has been popular throughout Europe. The cultural traditions of Austria found natural expression both in the development and the use of beautiful embroidery. Among these, the type known as Petit Point was most highly developed. It is a half cross stitch on an evenly woven screen, either gauze or canvas, worked in even lines from right to left, thus permitting a particularly rich combination of colors. It has become a favorite adornment for many articles, including shoes, handbags and dresses. Embroidery is done a great deal in the Spanish Ballearic Islands, on Teneriffe in the Canary Islands, and with particular distinction on the Portuguese island of Madeira, which is known for the perfection of its *festons,* or scalloped edges. Rumania and Hungary are well known for their own type of embroidery, called "peasant" work and characterized by simple folk designs on blouses and dresses of linen or cotton.

In England embroidery has been developed primarily as an avocation for ladies of leisure, rather than for commercial purposes. Some of the finest pieces ever made are on display in London's South Kensington Museum. Mary, Queen of Scots, Catherine of Aragon, Anne Boleyn and Queen Elizabeth were among the royal figures famous for their needlework, as is the Dowager Queen Mary today.

In the Philippine Islands and in Puerto Rico, to look at the other side of the embroidery picture, the craft has been the means of livelihood for many persons.

The beginning of today's embroidery industry may well be credited to Switzerland, and specifically to the famed embroidery workers of picturesque Appenzell and Innerhoden. Up to the early part of the present century they were a familiar sight in their native costumes, bending over embroidery frames in front of their chalet homes or behind clean windows.

Since early in the fourteenth century they had spun yarns and woven the finest cotton materials. When, early in the eighteenth century, yarns made in quantity by mechanical means came from England, they were forced to seek new fields in their struggle for existence and they chose embroidery by hand. With characteristic application, the women of Appenzell and Innerhoden soon brought a vital and practical contribution to the craft. Specializing in the use of white or blue yarns on fine materials, the Appenzellers embroidered clever designs with new stitches, skillfully executed with the finest yarns, and these found their way into public favor.

The city of St. Gall, well known as the maker and distributor of fine materials throughout the world, undertook to market the handwork of Appenzell and succeeded rapidly in building up a prosperous business. Over 1,500 workers, the heaviest concentration anywhere in Europe, were engaged in it. Each worker specialized in a particular type and quality. Skill, speed and care were the distinguishing accomplishments of Appenzell workers, and they earned compensation accordingly. Mothers taught their daughters, and eventually a school was founded by the federal government in 1889 and maintained by the Canton of Appenzell.

The heavy demand for fine articles of hand-embroidery in France induced considerable Swiss artisans at the beginning of the nineteenth century to join up with the workers of the Vosges Mountains. In an effort to enlarge their own clientèle for an ever-increasing output, Appenzell and Innerhoden sent women and girls in native costumes to summer and winter resorts to demonstrate to visitors the

No. 16C
APPENZELL WORKER MAKING EMBROIDERY
BY HAND

*Swiss worker making fine Appenzell Embroidery in white thread on
white material. The work is set on a frame.*
Courtesy APPENZELLERLAND, *Gais, Switzerland*

making of richly embroidered trousseaux, monogrammed handkerchiefs and table linen by hand.

Eventually, economic pressures caused extensive research look-
ing toward a machine to reproduce this handwork, for which there
was clearly a wide market waiting. A hand-loom machine was finally
developed. The key feature of this machine is the use of needles
with points at each end. This permits the thread to go through
the material from one side and then come right back again, and
results in exact replicas of certain types of hand-embroidery, including Beauvais, Petit Point and others. These hand-loom machines
were set up in homes throughout the region, thus founding a new
industry—embroidery by machine. As the price came down with
machine work, the market expanded rapidly, and St. Gall became
known as the "capital city" of embroidery.

Experiments continued and soon a further development was
achieved: a machine was built, the product of which was far more
varied than that of the hand-loom machine and proved to be the
final achievement in embroidery work.

This machine was called the Schiffli machine because the shuttle
in the back was in the shape of a little boat, for which the Swiss
diminutive is *schiffli*. The apparatus is ten to fifteen yards long. The
web of material to be embroidered is spanned firmly over a frame
which reaches the full length of the machine and which moves in
various directions, guided by a punched card. The needles, lined
up in a straight bank, move in and out and stitch the design on the
cloth. The modern machine is operated automatically. (Plate 33.)

Prosperity came quickly to the sponsors of the Schiffli embroidery
machine and Switzerland led vigorously in the further development
of this machine and its product. The greatest study, care and atten-
tion were applied to designing, enlarging the design, punching it
on the cards to guide the machine, developing accessories to bore
holes or eyelets, and finally, bleaching and dyeing.

The industry spread to Austria, Czechoslovakia and Saxony, and
reached large proportions. France, a little later, installed the Schiffli

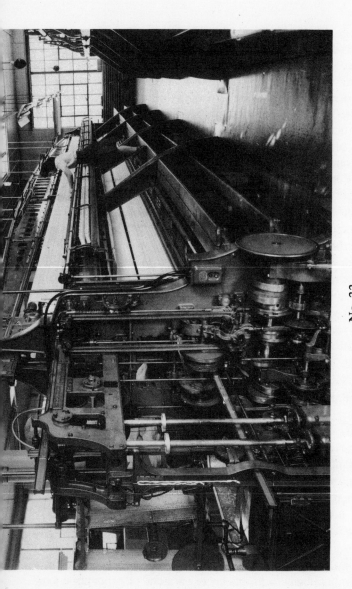

No. 33
SCHIFFLI EMBROIDERY MACHINE

This machine is operated automatically. The perforated roll of paper seen on the extreme left-hand side of the photograph automatically controls the movements of the needles which, in turn, produce the embroidered design on the material spanned across the machine.

Courtesy EMBROIDERY MFRS. BUREAU, INC.

machine in Caudry, Calais and St. Quentin, and Italy and other countries did likewise.

The discovery of the so-called "aetz" process enabled the Schiffli embroidery machine to produce laces. In this process the design is embroidered with cotton yarn on animal fiber, silk or wool. The animal fiber is later dissolved by a chemical bath, leaving only the airy lace design of cotton fiber. In this way the Schiffli machine produces principally reproductions of the famous Point Venice, Point Burano and Point Rose, and a large range called guipure laces, or Punta in Aria ("point in the air" in English, "luftspitzen" in German).

Another Schiffli machine product also joined the lace family. Nets, principally cotton, but also rayon and silk, are embroidered with cord or thread. These are known as Bretonne laces and the designs are similar to Alencon.

The varied output of the embroidery machine resulted in a substantial volume of exports from the principal producing countries, especially to America. Trimmings and appliques, yokes, embroidery edges in various widths, laces, ornamentation for handkerchiefs, wide eyelet allovers for dress material, motifs designed for pocketbooks, hats and shoes, in white and in colors, were readily designed and adjusted to meet new fads and fashions.

Early in the twentieth century nationals of the countries in which the industry had been established brought both the Schiffli machine and the hand-loom machine to America. The industry was launched along the eastern seaboard in close proximity to a style-conscious and constantly increasing clientèle.

The knowledge of designing, enlarging and punching designs for the automatic machine was brought here by Swiss experts. As a result of increased production and American enterprise, the industry in the United States thrived and expanded rapidly. Northern New Jersey has become the center of the American embroidery industry with about 400 firms operating 1,100 machines. Bleacheries, finishing plants and suppliers of yarn and other material swell the ranks of the industry. Thus imports were supplemented by domestic products readily accepted by the consumer.

HANDKERCHIEFS

There is hardly any other article which enters so intimately into our daily lives as the large range of handkerchiefs—plain, embroidered, or with lace borders.

Most popular is the handkerchief with embroidery, either daintily stitched in white, or more elaborately embroidered in colors, including the famous Petit Point and Beauvais stitch. China, Puerto Rico, Madeira, Spain, Switzerland, Italy and France are among the regions which enrich these squares of cotton or linen, either by hand or machine.

Sentiment and romance are attached to the handkerchief framed with lace. Bretonne Lace, Point Gaze, Point a l'Aiguille, Valenciennes, Alencon, Point de Rose, Carrickmacross and Duchesse are reproduced by machine and adorn the kind of handkerchief that is practically a symbol of a wedding, a graduation, a confirmation—the kind that stays in a family as a treasured memento. (Plates 6, 8, 8-A-B, 15, 32.)

No. 8A
HANDMADE CARRICKMACROSS

*The border of this handkerchief is handmade
and originated in Ireland.*
M. E. ABEL

No. 8B
SCHIFFLI MACHINE LACE BORDER

*The border on this handkerchief is a handmade reproduction
of Carrickmacross.*
M. E. ABEL

No. 32
CENTER HANDMADE ROSE POINT

*The border of this handkerchief is a Schiffli machine reproduction
of the handmade medallion in the center.*

M. E. ABEL

Research, A Tradition of the Industry

The continuous progress of lace and embroidery, as well as the preservation of artistic standards in their making, can be credited to the wealth of information available on these fabrics from the very beginning, and to the tireless research which has become a tradition in the industry. Today many of the world's museums, along with trade associations, are repositories of knowledge about lace.

The Gewerbe Museum in St. Gall, Switzerland, contains specimens of embroidery and lace from every period important from an historic, artistic or industrial point of view. Constant additions are made to this collection, including reference books with samples, designs and technical data. Younger designers and technicians derive from these new ideas which influence their work and provide new points of departure.

Italy's most valuable pieces are on display in churches, museums and the fine old homes of former owners. The educational approach of the lace projects on Burano and other places near Venice has helped preserve the Italian tradition.

Each year the *"Fete de la Dentelle"* has long been celebrated in Belgium, and until recently lace workers made pilgrimages to Hal, near Brussels, to offer a specially-made masterpiece to the "Lady of Hal." Through the years these offerings have accumulated, until now a large collection is preserved in the churches there as a monument to the skill of Belgian artisans. In Brussels the Royal Museum of Art and History has a good-sized lace collection, some of the pieces dating back as far as 1593.

In France research is pushed by the trade organizations, or *syndicales,* organized in each section where lace or embroidery is made. These sectional groups are joined under the banner of the "Lace Federation of France," with headquarters in Paris, where all aspects of the industry are studied on a national basis. The industries which use lace and embroidery, similarly organized, cooperate closely with the lace *syndicales.* As one example, take the most important of these consuming industries, the *haute couture* of Paris. The fashion designers are constantly thinking up new ways to use materials and new functions for old materials. Passed on to the lace people, these demands result in styles of audacity, logic and imagination.

The Lace Federation of France has founded *La Maison de la Dentelle et de la Broderie.* At its headquarters it is gathering specimens of lace and embroidery to be made available to students from all lands. In Paris, too, the *Musee des Arts Decoratifs* has a fine lace collection.

The Metropolitan Museum of Art in New York and the Boston Museum of Art have particularly beautiful collections of laces. The Morgan Collection, part of which is in New York and part in Boston, the Fahnestock Collection, and many others have been given to these museums for display. Exhibited in suitable settings, such collections can unquestionably increase public knowledge and appreciation of the art of lace and serve as inspirations to those who follow the craft, whether by hand or by machine.

In the United States the American Lace Manufacturers Association has played an important part in the rapid progress which has been achieved in the lace industry. American manufacturers have applied this country's mass production methods to the industry, and by close contact with consumers have increased interest in lace and embroidery. The Embroidery Manufacturers Bureau has guided the Schiffli embroidery industry which has also made great strides. The manufacture of embroideries permits rapid changes to adapt the product quickly to the fluctuating fashions that characterize the consuming public here. In the import field the Lace and

Embroidery Association of America is the guiding group on international trade activities. The Lowell Textile Institute, Lowell, Mass., offers a course in lace, and a recently established foundation provides a scholarship each year for some promising student.

Glossary

The first part of this booklet sought to give an historical background to help better to understand lace, to "feel" it.

The following section contains a catalogue of the various classifications under which embroidery and lace fabrics are grouped, and a description of many modern laces, their names, distinctions and uses.

The names of laces derive from many sources. In most cases a lace has been called by the name of the town or region where it was first produced, or where a lace has been made particularly well over a long period of time.

Sometimes the name refers to the place where it found greatest favor. Point d'Angleterre, for example, was applied to some laces just because they were very popular in England.

Whatever the reason, the names by which laces are known have stuck to them, so that even in the rush of modern times, the romantic old syllables still carry meaning and importance. Nowadays, to be sure, when the names are used they apply usually to the type of "real" lace being duplicated by machine.

Terms

Beading Edges: Applies to lace or embroidery. Edge with holes through which a ribbon can be drawn either to achieve a ruffled effect or to serve as added adornment.

Beading Galloon: Applies to lace or embroidery. Band with scalloped edge on each side in a variety of widths, with holes in center, permitting ribbon to go through for shoulder straps on camisoles, lingerie, and also for adorning dresses. (Plate 17-C.)

Beading Insertions: Applies to lace or embroidery. Straight edge on both sides and slits in the center to put ribbon through. Used for babywear, underwear, children's dresses, carriage covers, shoulder straps on camisoles and lingerie, etc., and for the purpose of pulling the material when ruffled effects are to be achieved. (Plate 17-A.)

Camisoles: Beading on top of either lace or embroidery edge to wear under sheer materials. Widths from 2 inches to 12 inches.

Cordonnet: The thread or cord outlining a lace design.

Edges, Flounces: Lace or embroidery. Straight on one side with scalloped edge on the other side. Width from ½ inch to 36 inches. In all classes and types. (Plates 17-E, 28-B-C-E, 18, 19, 21, etc.)

Embroidery Allovers: 36 inches or wider. The design embroidered over the full width of the material: linen, pique, organdy, cotton, rayon, silk and nylon without scallops on either side, made in white, pastel and street shades. Used for dress materials and on pillow covers, for blouses, and other articles. (Plate 26.)

Galloons: Lace or embroidery with scalloped edge on both sides. Widths from ½ inch to 10 inches. Embroidery or lace. (Plates 27-A-C-D, 28-A, 29-A, 20-B, 22-B, 23-A.)

Incrustations, Medallions, Motifs: Distinct designs, pre-made or cut from the lace. The light types are set in by hand on lingerie and the heavier types are used to add ornamentation on many articles of household or other uses. (Center Plate 10.)

Insertions: Applies to lace or embroidery. Inserted, as name implies, to join two pieces of fabrics together. Each side is straight and reinforced with extra threads to facilitate sewing and give added strength. (Plates 28-D, 29-B, 17-D.)

Lace Allovers: 36 inches or wider, without scallops on either side, the design spread over the entire width. Comes in large range of types and shades, and used as material for day and evening dresses. (Plates 24, 30, 31.)

Toile: The heavy filling or pattern of a lace design as distinguished from the background.

Veinings: Also called *Entredeux*. Used to join various parts of materials, thus serving utilitarian and ornamental purposes. Widths from ⅛ inch to ½ inch.

Vraie: French word to designate a lace as "real" or handmade.

Types

Alencon Lace: Made by hand in Alencon, France, during the early part of the sixteenth century. This lace marked the beginning of the whole series of delicate, light French laces which earned instant favor. It was used to cover altars, to trim surplices, to make cravats, fans, handkerchiefs and ruffles for the ladies and gentlemen of the court. Beautiful pieces exist throughout museums of the world. It is easily distinguished by a "cordonnet" or heavy thread which outlines the design, usually floral, on a fine net background. (Plate 9.) It is perfectly reproduced on the Leavers machine in France, England and the U. S. A. The lowered price has multiplied its use to large proportions. It wears and washes unusually well and is used generously and skillfully on lingerie and negligees and also to embellish dresses, pillows, baby covers, household and boudoir articles. Comes in edges, bands, galloons and incrustations from 1½ inches to 10 inches and also in 36-inch allovers. (Plates 21, 22, 23.)

Altar Lace: A name applied to laces of any type used for church decorations upon the altar or for vestments. Designs are largely of medieval or religious inspiration, in widths from 3 up to 45 inches.

Appliqué Lace or Point Appliqué: A design separately cut, hand applied to another material, skillfully atached to a background which is most frequently net, also made by machine.

Argentan Lace: A needlepoint lace which originated in Argentan, France, and is very similar to Alencon lace and like the latter, originally called "Point de France." Designs still made in Argentan are larger and bolder than Point Alencon and less expensive. (Plate 10, 11.) It is reproduced by machine and serves the same purposes as Alencon lace.

Argentella Point Lace: The result of an attempt by Italy to make light and fine laces in Burano. It resembles Argentan and Alencon laces.

Baby Irish: A lace which is of a crochet character made by hand in widths up to 4 inches. It originated in Ireland, but was eventually made in very large quantities in China. Its use is very large for garments of every description. (Plate 18-F and G.)

Baby Lace: A term for very narrow light laces, principally Valenciennes, Cluny or Crochet. (Plate 17-B and E.)

Barmen Lace: Named after a city in Germany. Machine-made reproductions of hand made French and Belgian Torchons and Clunys.

Binche Lace: Hand-made Binche lace came from the Town of Hainault in Flanders. It is a cotton lace distinguished by its fancy net or ground, sometimes a "fond de neige" (snow) and belongs to the Valenciennes family. Reproductions are made by machine in France, England and the U. S. A. Its uses are the same as Valenciennes where a more conspicuous type of lace is preferred. (Plate 17-H.)

Bobbinet: A net made with bobbins. Whereas it was formerly made with the needle by hand, it is now produced by machine of cotton, rayon, nylon or silk. The finer nets are called tulle. Its use is very large for dresses and trimmings.

Bretonne Lace: Appears to have originated as a hand-made lace in Brittany. It is now made on the Schiffli embroidery machine, but the net background puts it into the lace category. Comes in edges and galloons up to 18-inch and 20-inch widths, and allovers up to 72 inches, and is used for lingerie, blouses, dresses, yokes, pillow covers, handkerchief borders, and a variety of articles. (Plate 29-A.)

Bruges Lace: Named after Bruges, Belgium. A bobbin lace similar to Binche, but of a different background.

Burano Lace: Burano is an island near Venice, Italy, renowned for its hand production of Point Venice and eventually of lighter laces. The name is applied to its products.

Burnt-Out Lace: A design stitched with cotton on an animal fibre, generally silk. The latter is eventually removed by an acid bath leaving the airy embroidery as lace. It reproduces the original Italian *Punto in Aria,* (German *Luftspitzen,* "points in the air.") It is commercially known as Venice or Guipure type and is used for trimming heavy materials, such as velvet and satins, as well as light materials, such as silks and cotton. (Plate 25.)

Carrickmacross Lace: A hand-made lace originating in Ireland which achieved high favor. It could almost be called an embroidery, being an applique applied upon a background, generally net. Sometimes the design is also a guipure type treated in the same manner. (Plate 8-A-B.)

Chantilly Lace: Its beginning dates from the first half of the eighteenth century when it was made by hand in Chantilly, France. It is reported to have been the favorite lace of Madame DuBarry and Marie Antoinette. It was characterized by fine ground and elegance of floral patterns, with toile of silk with cotton or linen cordonnet. (Plate 13.) No hand-made lace is now made in Chantilly and machinery has taken over the making of this beautiful lace. France has exhibited great skill in drawing the complex Chantilly designs, and care in the clipping and finishing of these designs. It is also made in England and America, particularly in 36-inch allovers which have grown to be a favorite and very rich material for negligees and dinner, bridal and evening gowns. (Plates 24, 30, 31.) Made in all widths from ½ inch up, it is a type of lace which lends itself especially well to colors. (Plate 20.)

Cluny Lace: A coarse, strong lace still made by hand in LePuy, France, and in Belgium and China. Its name was taken from the Cluny Museum in Paris. (Plate 18-E.) It is also made by machine. Formerly it was made of linen, but now almost entirely of cotton, except some of the real types. Imitations are produced which simulate these effects on machine. (Plate 29-B.)

Crochet Lace: Originally introduced in Ireland about 1820, it eventually became a very large industry in the neighborhood of Cork. The Austrian government subsequently made the manufacture of this lace into a national industry employing large numbers of workers. It imitates a very narrow Venice type. While reproductions are made by machine, Belgium, Italy, France and particularly China, continue the production of this lace by hand. In all widths, starting from ¼ inch. (Plate 18-A-B-C.)

Duchesse Lace: A light lace with tape-like characteristics formerly made by hand in Flanders and Italy. (Border Plate 6.) Now made partly by hand by combining machine-made tape with very light guipure effect. Reproductions are made with a very fine thread on the embroidery and the Leavers machines. (Plate 25-A-B.)

Ecclesiastical Lace: Any of many laces specially designed and used for church purposes.

Filet Lace: Square meshes with the squares partly filled in to form the design.

LePuy Laces: One of the old centers of lace-making in France. Formerly Le Puy laces were made entirely by hand, but in recent years they are also made by machines, producing particularly the Crochet, Torchon and Cluny types.

Macrame Lace: One of the oldest laces, a heavy Venice type, made by machine now and used where heavy lace is required.

Maline Lace: Characterized by small pretty floral designs on fine net ground. A light lace taking its name from the town in Belgium in which it was originally made by hand. Now reproduced by machine in Calais and Caudry, France, and to a lesser extent in Nottingham, England. (Plate 19-B.)

Mechlin Lace: Another type of Valencienne lace of very fine yarn and fine mesh with a slightly heavier cordonnet forming the design. (Plate 14.) It is now reproduced by machine.

Milan Point: Originated in the sixteenth century in Italy. Used as a trade term for a lace made by hand with the use of a machine-made braid produced principally in Belgium. (Plate 5.) Similar types are made by machine.

Nottingham: Town in England where laces are made. The name is applied to many types of the Valenciennes family.

Picot Lace: A finishing lace of narrow loops, round or triangular-shaped. (Plate 18-A-B-C.)

Point D'Angleterre or English Point: A lace made by hand in Brussels and in England. In the latter country it found particularly great favor, but the largest supply came from Flanders.

Point D'Esprit: A net band from ½ inch to 6 inches with dots covering the entire width and up to 72 inches as a member of the net family.

Point Lille: Originally created by hand near Lille, France, on a hexagonal background and with very fine yarn. A member of the Valenciennes family, its background is often filled in with dots between the heavy, well-defined but small designs. Now also made by machine.

Point De Paris (Normandy Lace): Originally made as a reasonably priced, hand-made lace in Normandy and Paris. (Plate 15 border.) Has a light open background mesh with a sharply-defined pattern of flowers. It comes in widths of 1 to 3 inches, produced now by machine (Plate 19-C) referred to as **Calais Vals.** It is a solid lace adaptable to lingerie and many other purposes where a wider and more showy lace than Valencienne is required.

Princess Lace: A very cleverly made imitation of Duchesse lace, being made of a machine-made braid or very narrow flat Valenciennes lace hand-wrought into a very delicate lace, joining the various parts together.

Rosaline (Petites Roses): Little roses worked in Venice type, very light. (Plate 3.) Also reproduced on the Schiffli embroidery machine.

Shadow Lace: A thin lace, made on the Leavers machine, of a shadowy design; used today largely for background for re-embroidery.

Torchons: Plain designs, less lacy appearance, made with fairly heavy yarn in widths from 1 to 3 inches.

Valenciennes Laces ("Vals"): This best known and easily distinguishable lace was originally made by hand in Valenciennes, France, with linen threads. It has a net ground with either diamond-shaped or round holes; the toile or design is flat and sheer, and usually flowered. It is now entirely made of cotton. Plate 18-D, 15.) While still made by hand in Belgium and China, it is one of the first laces made successfully by machine. It became a practical and large business by 1834, when Calais and Caudry, France, and Nottingham, England, became the centers of its early manufacture, followed by the U. S. A. Its simplicity is particularly appealing and it is freely used on babywear, lingerie, neckwear, dresses, hats, boudoir and household articles in many varied widths, of which the most popular are the narrow sizes up to 1½ inches. (Plates 17, 19-A.)

Venice Lace: Originally made by hand in Venice, Italy, divided into various classifications, Gros Point being the heavier form and Rose Point the lighter. (Plate 32.) Other types are called Venice Plat and Venice Relief, all of great renown. (Plates 1, 2.) They are reproduced by machine in a wide variety of designs in edges and galloons of various widths. Venice types are also made as wide allovers and used for yokes on dresses, sleeves and shoulders, or as inserts on dresses. The insertions and edges are used to trim heavy and light materials, such as satins and velvets, and silks and cottons. (Plate 25.)

Point De Gaze: Needlepoint lace made in Brussels. (Plates 7, 8.) Reproduced by machine, a combination of net embroidered with fine yarn (Border Plate 32.)

*   *   *

The laces mentioned in the foregoing glossary are primarily those which are still in use and in parlance today. Most of them are now made by machine. There are other laces, important to history and art, but not to the present commercial scene. Some of the names are:

Devonshire Lace: Lace-making began in Devonshire, England, about 1685. The first results were coarse, but the lace was later improved and for a time resembled similar Flemish types.

Dutch Lace: A class of bobbin laces once made in Holland—generally coarser imitations of French or Belgian laces.

Honiton: British type in which bobbin-made motifs were joined by needle, in imitation of certain Belgian laces, especially Duchesse type.

Limerick: A nineteenth-century Irish cross between lace and embroidery applique, with openwork design on a net background.

Point à l'Aiguille: Old French term for needlepoint laces, some of which are still made.

Point de Brabant: The same as Point de Bruxelles.

Point de Bruxelles: Term for needlepoint or bobbin laces made in Brussels and environs.

Point de Colbert: Venice type laces when first made in France were named in honor of Colbert, French Minister of Finance, who favored lace.

Point d'Espagne: A heavy lace made in Spain around the sixteenth century.

Point de Genes: One of the very early developments of lace in Genoa, later improved on by Venice.

Reticella Lace: An early needlepoint lace employing classic geometric designs.

No. 17

LEAVERS

VALENCIENNES

*Valenciennes are made on the
Leavers machine in various
qualities, depending upon
fineness of yarn and the gauge
of the machine. A to F,
Diamond mesh ground; G,
round mesh ground; H, snow
mesh Binche ground.*

A

B

C

D

E

F

G

H

No. 18

MODERN

HANDMADES

*These samples are Chinese;
similar laces are made in Italy
and Ireland. A to C, Picot
edges. D, Valenciennes;
E, Cluny; F and G, Irish-type
crochet.*

A

B

C

D

E

F

G

No. 19

LEAVERS

MACHINE

VALENCIENNES

*A, Ground mesh Valenciennes
with muslin effect; B, Mechlin
type lace with diamond mesh
and fine flowers; C, Calais
Val, also called Nottingham or
Normandy lace.*

A

B

C

No. 20

LEAVERS

CHANTILLY

Chantilly is made by machine with silk, cotton and rayon yarn—silk chief value. A fine pattern edge; B, Applique imitation; C, Chantilly with heavier designs.

No. 21

LEAVERS

MACHINE

ALENCON

A and B, Alencon type with fine cotton yarn; C, Alencon type with nylon yarn.

A

B

No. 22

LEAVERS

ALENCON

*A and B, Alencon type edges
reproduced by machine
from the real.*

No. 23

HAND-RUN

ALENCON

*The outline is applied by the
Pusher machine operated
by hand. This closest
reproduction of the handmade
is produced principally in
Lyons, France.*

No. 24

CHANTILLY

APPLIQUE

*Allover pattern, 36" wide,
used for bridal gowns,
produced on the Leavers
machine.*

No. 25

VENICE

LACE

These copies were made on the Schiffli machine. A and B, flat Duchesse effect, edges; C, heavy (Gros Point) Venice edge; D, heavy (Gros Point) Venice galloon (also called Guipure lace).

A

B

C

D

No. 26

EMBROIDERY

ALLOVER

Embroidery design repeated over the entire width of 40" on organdy. It is also made on pique, nylon, batiste and other materials.

No. 27

SCHIFFLI

MACHINE

EMBROIDERIES

A and B, Edge and galloon embroidered on batiste novelty effects. Holes made by borers as part of machine operation; C and D, edge and galloon with cut-out effect on organdy, cutting done by hand.

A

B

C

D

No. 28

SCHIFFLI

MACHINE

EMBROIDERIES

Designs and patterns typical of everyday embroideries, which are made up to 10" widths. These are often called "broderies anglaises."

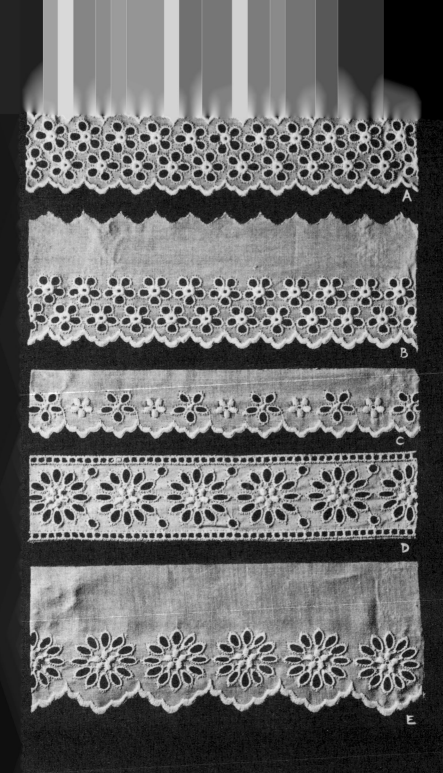

No. 29

MACHINE

LACES

A, Bretonne lace made on the Schiffli machine, embroidered on net; B, Cluny lace insertion (also comes in edges), made with cheap cotton yarn on the Barmen machine.

A

B

No. 30

LEAVERS

MACHINE

CHANTILLY

Duchess effect, design made with fine yarn, silk, rayon and cotton—silk chief value.

No. 31

LEAVERS

MACHINE

CHANTILLY

*Chantilly made with very fine
yarn—silk, rayon and
cotton, silk chief value.
Of very light, fine texture
and design.*